IN THE ZONE

BY
THE MENTAL TRADER

Click the QR to join me on twitter for daily inspiration and guidance to help you become a better sports trader.

https://twitter.com/thementaltrader

August 2005.

Before starting trading, he'd been a regular punter for over thirty years. Betting nearly every day, he only used small stakes, and he didn't keep any records of his bets. He didn't need to know how profitable or not he actually was. He only placed bets for fun, so he thought it wasn't worth the time recording them and it was time consuming. Over the last few weeks and months, he guessed that he had been losing more than winning and it was becoming irritating. He could feel that he was becoming obsessed with trading and the thought of making a comfortable living easily. He decided he had to look into it seriously. Having read so much about it in online forums and on Facebook, he opened an account with Betfair and searched for every snippet of info that he could find about trading sports.

All he read told him that being able to lay and back horses, meant it was now very easy to make decent, regular profits. Lots of ordinary people were making enormous sums and a large percentage were doing it in their pyjamas in front of their PC.

He went all in with learning to trade. He spent several months selling anything and everything he could on eBay to accumulate a betting bank.

He had read that successful traders kept their betting money separate from his other cash, so that is what he did.

He knew that his wife had too many pairs of shoes, so he sold a lot of them. She didn't notice. After a couple of months, he had built up a bank of £1000.

This was it, this was his passport to financial freedom and a life of doing something that he loved for the rest of his days. To begin with, it all went very well. He was making small but regular profits of about £2 per race with very little risk, and making the right trading choices seemed simple. His stakes were around £10 or £15 and that was quite comfortable for him. He fantasised about scaling this up and doing it for a living. He dreamt of sitting on a sun kissed beach, drink by his side and getting a tan while trading, all with no boss that he hated to tell him what to do.

It wasn't all plain sailing. On a couple of occasions, he had placed trades that he should have exited way before he actually did, and he was very lucky to have got away with a minimal loss, or sometimes even a win after letting them go in play. He knew he couldn't carry on doing that or else the profits that he had patiently built up would vanish. Each time, he swore never to do it again. It was bad for his nerves. After a few weeks, the betting bank balance had risen to £2000. He still found himself unprepared in some situations and taking unnecessary risks by going in-play, but this was now becoming much less frequent. It was usually when he was panicking and there was a very real chance of a big pre race loss

That was when his equilibrium would falter. He'd taken a couple of hefty losses of around £100, but his bank could take that. Even though it did really get him down when it first happened, he managed to stay positive most of the time and would give himself a couple of days to regroup, then come back again, more determined, albeit with a reduced betting bank.

Then on one very normal midweek racing day it all went wrong.

He had a powerful conviction that a horse would not win.
This conviction was not based on anything other than the way the horses price was fluctuating in the betting markets. It had been long 'odds on' with the morning tissue prices and by dinner time it was trading at even money.
"There's no way on earth that it's going to win now," he thought. The market and obviously the people in the know were against the horse. They were obviously lumping sizeable sums against it, and if he joined them, it was nailed on to be profitable for him too.

He had laid it early in the day for small amounts at 1.7 and was now thinking about laying again at evens. If he had really thought about it, he could have taken a nice profit by backing the horse at evens, rather than laying it again, but he had convinced himself that it would lose. So he laid more cash against it.

As the race got nearer, the more uneasy he became. The horse was now being backed to win. In the normally accurate betting forecast in the Racing Post it was priced at 3/10.

"It will probably come in a bit in the betting, but surely it won't hit 1.33, not after drifting to evens."

That assumption proved false. Its price kept getting shorter. 1.8, 1.7, 1.6, 1.5. He was now looking at a substantial loss if he got out of the bet now.

"I'll leave it," he thought, "surely it will drift back out again soon."

Wrong again, 1.45, 1.4, 1.35 and it was still being backed.

This was now confusing.

"I'm going to lay this again, ready for when it slides," he thought.

He clicked the lay side and put in a stake of £500 at 1.4, adding more liability to his already precarious position.

As the money to back the horse kept appearing on the exchange, he had another thought.

"I'll go in play and hope it gets a slow start, then I'll get out of the trade as soon as I am in a better position."

"What about your promise never to go in-play again?" another part of his mind asked.

He ignored that question.

Race time arrived, so he opened the video feed on Betfair; he was sweating and silently praying that his horse, in stall two, would be the last horse to emerge when the stalls opened.

His horse was now at 1.3 and he was bricking it.

SUSPENDED came up across the computer screen in big letters. Staring at stall two on the video, he breathed a sigh of relief as the horse broke only adequately.

At least it hadn't made a rapid start and gone clear. The race was being run over 12 furlongs, and he did his best to watch the prices and the horse at the same time. Its odds were 1.35, and it was in third. It looked to be travelling easily, but he agreed with himself to leave it a little longer to get more of a profit when it faded.

"Just a bit longer," he thought. He didn't have a time span or an amount of money that he was happy to lose to exit the trade associated with "a bit longer". He was winging it, stuck in a sort of no-man's-land and he had little idea about what to do.

The fact was, he was ill prepared for this situation at all.

"Time to get out, that's enough, exit," he thought. He was going to lose, but to hell with it. He had somehow admitted he didn't have a clue what he was doing, so he needed to do something.

He clicked his cursor on the price button. His computer screen locked. He bashed the keys with both palms, but nothing happened. It had completely frozen. The price of his horse on the screen when it locked was 1.5.

"Surely it was drifting as it was dropping back and out of contention," he thought with his fingers and toes firmly crossed.

The betting screen came back on, but not the video or audio. The price was now 1.25, and his liability was £1000, then it went to 1.2 for more of a loss.

He wasn't even remotely religious, but he prayed. "Please, please, please get beaten," was his plea.

He made a promise to himself and whoever else was listening.

"If I get out of this one I will never, ever go in play again, and that's a promise."

He continued to stare at the screen. 1.15, 1.1, 1.09. Down and down the price went. Then it hit 1.01, and the big SUSPENDED appeared across the screen again. This time, there was no chance of a reprieve. All hope had gone. Staring at the digits 1.01 on the screen, he felt sick. He was sweating and hoping against hope that the market would miraculously open again and give him the chance to get his money back, but of course it didn't.

"Maybe there'll be a steward's enquiry," was his last thought. That was another forlorn hope. He put his head in his hands and looked at the red figure against the winner. -£1,800. He felt sick. All that work, all that saving and all that cash gone in just a few minutes.

Writing that brought back the pain. It is the story of my first foray into trading and it taught me several very harsh, painful lessons. On the bright side, it also encouraged me to look into the psychological side of trading and to figure out a little more about how I could enjoy myself whilst doing it.

I began to realise that to make it as a successful sports trader you need a balanced view of the markets, and a whole different set of skills than a gambler.

Once I had regained my equilibrium, which took quite a while, I had gained a new determination to never again feel as bad as I did that day. So I started working on myself. That is an ongoing project, and gets more enjoyable the more I do it.

I hope I can help any sports trader that reads my words to become a better trading person both in the markets and in everyday life and to help avoid making the same mistakes that I did.
Realising quickly that your biggest obstacle to success is your own thinking means things become a lot easier a lot faster.

Some people will say that the hard times help you really appreciate the good, and I mostly agree with that, but whilst no one will ever be able to stop anyone else from completely cutting out every bad habit, I hope I can help lessen the frequency of them.

If this book helps even a little, then it will have been worth writing.

Foreword

I am honoured to be asked to write this foreword for such an outstanding fella as the Mental Trader. I have known Paul for over fifty years and can say that, like a fine wine, he has improved with age. I have followed his trading career from the early days of the betting exchanges to the present, and enjoyed watching him progress from a guesser who picked his trades using nothing more than intuition and a wing and a prayer, to a trader that is level-headed and decides on his trades based on sound logic. I can say without fear of contradiction that anyone who takes the time to read his words and digest the nuggets in this book will succeed.

No more downward spirals after an avoidable loss and pure elation after an excellent decision and large profit. Trading will become so much more simple and enjoyable without the hard work and grind.

Paul is an all round top guy, and it is a pleasure to have watched him develop into such a first class human being.

Enjoy reading how he did it, follow his advice and become just like him, almost perfect.

All the best,

Paul, The Mental Trader.

How did you feel when you read the foreword?

Surely that can't be serious?

Wow, this guy must be the bee's knees. I will read his every word and be like him?

Did you think, what an arsehole?

Were you tempted to stop reading straight away and dismiss the book as nonsense?

Did you want to jump in and find out what made me so good?

I wrote that foreword myself for a good reason. To prove how our thinking creates our reality.

Whether you think I am a narcissist who loves himself, an idiot who doesn't know what he's talking about, or whether you just want to know what else I have to say, remember that they are all just thoughts. Opinions that are your own. They have nothing to do with the words that you read.

If that was the case, everyone would react in the same way to those words, but they don't.

What the chuff has this got to do with sports trading, you might ask?

Well, I hope to point you to another way of looking at how you trade and how you react to, and what you expect from your trading.

Hopefully, on the way I can help you become more successful. Not using the traditional measures of success. These can be deceiving.

People can have lots of money and appear to have a perfect life, even though they may live in a constant state of despair. Sometimes people who look like they don't have a pot to pee in may be the happiest people alive.

I want to point you towards a different way of looking at life and help you become a more level-headed and happier trader.

Thanks for not closing the book already.

Introduction

"Never forget that trading should be fun. If you don't enjoy it, why do it?"

This is not an instruction book. It is more of a book of insights that I have had, that have helped me see trading in a totally different way to when I first started.
I have learned some very valuable lessons over the years and I'm hoping that I can pass some on to you.
 It isn't filled with techniques that will transform you if you follow them to the letter.

My intent is that sharing what has appeared to me can spark insights in you. Maybe they can show you a different way of trading and how we all create our own reality about the markets and life.

There is a common consensus in the trading fraternity that only a tiny proportion of sports traders are successful in the long term.
Its seems like the "hardest way to make an easy living," is spot on.

It may be true that there are very few profitable traders and it takes years to become a success, it may not be true too.

Your starting point on the trading journey can seem either difficult or easy in accordance with your thoughts about the statement above.

It is totally unprovable one way or the other, but if you take it to be true, then you may well expect to struggle from the outset and could be disheartened more quickly.

It would be easy to fall into the trap of thinking, if very few people do actually make it as profitable traders, why should I be any different? And so give up at the first hurdle.

I would suggest that viewing the statement as false would be much better for your own journey.
It's impossible to know how many traders actually try and fail to make it their livelihood, so why not assume that it's easy to be successful. That way of thinking is much more likely to help, rather than hinder you.

Some people seem to be able to make life changing decisions in an instant while others dither and fart about for years and get nowhere.
What is it that accounts for all the miraculous changes in peoples lives that we see?
The 350lb person that lost half their body weight in a year and is now a new person. The chain smoker who woke up one day and decided that they had had enough of smoking and stopped their 60 a day habit immediately and never smoked again.

The people that do these kinds of things are no different than any other person on the planet. They all just had a new thought about their life and it changed without effort. We are all capable of this and it doesn't matter how unrealistic it looks to you at the present moment. Changes like the above can and will happen to you if you make that decision.

What separates these apparent super humans from everyone else?

- Were they born with some innate quality of thinking that most people weren't?
- Do they have a different brain structure than everyone else?
- Do they have a different way of looking at the world?
- Have they got balls of steel and a cast iron will?
- Have more faith in their judgement?

I do not know for sure, but my best guess would be that they gave no thought to failure. They may not even be aware of that, but I would wager that this is the difference that makes a big difference between long term success in the sports markets and not. Don't make failure an option.

My aim in this book is to help you see a new way of viewing the world and your trading and to help you open up to a new way of being that will make a massive difference to your life.

My aim with this book is to help you see a new way of viewing the world and your trading and to help you open up to a new way of being that will make a massive difference to your life.

I would like to ask you to read this book with an open mind. I know that some of the ideas that I am going to present may seem a bit odd when compared to other trading psychology books. I will touch on the ideas that most people see as important to successful trading. Self control and discipline, bank management, etc, but I will approach these in a way that may be new to you. Some may seem like they have very little to do with making profits, but I would ask you to suspend those opinions to start with.

There are no trading strategies here.

There are plenty of books already available which take you through the why's and wherefores of picking your selections, what triggers to look for and how to find an edge. I would argue that your peace of mind is the biggest edge you have and once you see this, trading gets easier and more enjoyable.

"If you are trying to quieten your mind by not thinking, STOP!
When you are trying not to think, you are actually thinking more than when you're not thinking about not thinking.
Thinking is the problem, not the thoughts."

Before I go any further I would like to ask you to read my words in a slightly different way than you normally do. I know that might seem like a strange request, but bear with me. Most of the time we read for entertainment or for information about how to solve a particular problem. This book is different. It doesn't contain any magic mantras or techniques, I know that you don't need them and by the end of this book I hope to show you the truth of that, even if you might think I am bonkers now.

Try and forget what you know about how the mind works, your opinions about self help, and even what you think is true about how the world works, how you think and how you form your opinions.

I'm not going to try and change any of your thinking, I am hopefully going to show you that there is a new way of looking at life and that it can help you in any area and can make a massive difference to your sports trading. So read and try to not judge what you read against what you already know.

When we are born we are a completely blank slate. Our thinking about the world and our opinions start to form the minute we appear in the world, there's even evidence that they start to form whilst we are still in our mothers womb.
(See Bruce Lipton's excellent book, The Biology Of Belief.)

There are thousands of self help books and self improvement techniques in print and online that promise to help you get better at managing your emotions. They promise that if you practice such and such a technique your life will improve in leaps and bounds. This book is different. It starts with the assumption that your mindset does not need improving, or that your thinking is wrong in some kind of way and that if you follow what I say you will become a much better thinker and be able to make perfect decisions about markets and odds. Thinking is not something that we have much control over. When I really began to see that, my life improved in all areas.

What I hope my words will help you see is that we always have the choice about what we believe to be true. Just because you have thought a particular way for what seems like your whole life, it doesn't mean that you can't suddenly think the opposite. Your life can change exponentially after one new thought. We are all different and we all have our own opinions and nobody elses are any better than yours. They are all unique. There are approximately 7 billion realities in the world and yours is just one of them.

The fundamental premise of this book is:

YOU DO NOT NEED TO THINK DIFFERENTLY OR CHANGE YOUR MINDSET TO BECOME A BETTER TRADER. ITS A LOT SIMPLER THAN THAT.

Feelings

"The emotionally intelligent person is skilled in four areas; identifying emotions, using emotions, understanding emotions, and regulating emotions." – **John Mayer**

How you feel when you sit down to trade is vital to how your session will go.

Your expectations can cause havoc. You may have thought you had a good day yesterday, and so you will try to have an even better one today.

You may think that you had a terrible day yesterday and need to get your losses back today. Neither viewpoint is at all conducive to balanced and level-headed trading. Trade without restriction by forgetting completely about winning and losing. Profit and loss are irrelevant at any single moment. What matters most is whether you have followed your trading plan.

Which scenario would you prefer, following your process and taking a slight loss, or not following your process and winning a little? I would suggest that the former is the one to aim for. That is based on sound logic. The second is pure luck.

Take a look at the following two scenarios.

1.

You are lying in bed. It's 3.30 am and you have
been woken three times in three hours, by
your neighbours loud music, cats fighting on
the lawn below your bedroom window and a
noisy police helicopter. It seems to hover over
your roof with its search light illuminating
your room. They are probably looking out for
the local drug addicts who congregate at the
corner of your road. You need to get up in
three hours as you have an important meeting,
a two-hour drive from your usual base. Why
do these things always happen when you so
badly need to sleep? I'll be tired later on in the
day and the long journey home after the
meeting will be dreadful. You lay there,
mulling these things over for what seems like
hours before finally dropping off to sleep 30
minutes before your alarm clock goes off.
When it sounds, you lay still, mentally running
through how your day is going to turn out. It
will be a disaster. You are so tired. The
neighbours, their cats and the police have
caused you to miss your sleep. You jump out of
bed when the clock says 5.45am and step
straight on a lego brick, left there last night by
your son. It's like standing on a nail and as you
hop nearer to the bathroom cursing and
screaming, under your breath, so as not to
wake your other half who is still sleeping like a
log, you bang your toe on the bathroom
doorjamb. When you finally get into the
bathroom, you look at your watch and it's
6.15am, much later than you wanted to get up.

The battery in your alarm clock must be dying. So now you are rushing.

You don't think you'll have time for breakfast now, so you have a record breaking fast shower, get dressed, rush downstairs like a ninja, and grab a bottle of water and banana from the fridge on your way out to the car. As you put your key in the ignition, the top comes off the water bottle and spills the contents down the leg of your trousers. Now you look like you have been incontinent. After a hasty change of pants, you jump into your car, turn the key and all you hear is a click. The battery is flat. You call the breakdown service who come and get you going again but not before a half hour wait for them to arrive, in which you have sat there thinking about how late you are going to be for your meeting and how agitated your boss will be.

Finally arriving at the venue, flustered beyond description at 9.45 am, having driven like a maniac through the traffic that seemed much busier than normal.

You now think that you'll probably get a speeding ticket in the post in a day or two. You should have been sat down and ready by 8.45am and your boss, who lives even further away than you, is giving you an evil stare as you burst in. It is going to be a long day.

2.

You are lying in bed. It's 3.30 am. You have
heard the neighbours' music playing twice
during the night and also their cats have been
having what sounds like a rave on the lawn
below your window. A police helicopter seems
to hover over your roof with its search light
illuminating your room. You hope that
whoever they are looking for is ok. Each time
you have woken, you have taken some deep
breaths and immediately gone back to sleep
after putting on headphones, closing your eyes
and listening to some nice relaxing music on
your phone. You know you need to be up and
out of bed by 6.00 am so you went to bed at
9.30pm last night as you know that you
usually need at least seven hours of quality
sleep to be at your best. Tomorrow is an
important day, so you do all you can to be
ready for it. When the alarm clock rings, you
jump up immediately and sit on the side of the
bed for a moment, rubbing your eyes and
getting your bearings. You spot a rogue piece
of lego on the floor and put it on the dressing
table. You take off your watch and get a jolt
when you see it is 6.15am, the battery in the
clock must be flat. Never mind, you jump
straight into the shower and give yourself a
few minutes to just stand under the water and
consciously relax. Experience has taught you
that when you feel yourself getting agitated, it
is best to slow down. Your previous default
setting was to speed up.

You take some deep breaths as the water cascades over you. You decide to grab a water and banana on your way out. When you get in your car at 6.30am, you turn the key and hear the click of a dead battery. The top comes off the water bottle and spills down the leg of your trousers. No worries, the trousers will dry during the journey. You ring your boss and leave them a voice message telling them you may be a little late because of the dead battery and you'll be there as quick as you can. After ringing the breakdown service, you go over your notes about the meeting and listen to an audio-book that you have been meaning to listen to for a while. The traffic on the journey is quite busy, but you stay calm as you know there isn't any point in getting agitated, there's nothing you can do about it so you enjoy listening to your book as you drive as fast as you legally can and arrive at the venue at 9.45am. You walk in calmly and your manager greets you with a smile. It is going to be a good day.

The two scenarios above have exactly the same outside circumstances, but two totally different personal reactions. One means a lot of personal heartache and terrible feelings, the other has a much calmer feel and will make for a much easier day. This is down to perspective. It is such a simple thing to be prepared, but one we often ignore. If we transfer this to trading, it's easier to see that if we prepare in advance, we are much more likely to have a pleasant experience in the markets.

What Is Your Why?

"Why is Monday so far from Friday, and Friday so near to Monday?"

Why do you trade on sports? What do you enjoy about it?

What keeps you doing it?

How do you think your life will improve because of it?

Do you really want to trade for a living?

Or do you want the lifestyle that you imagine goes with trading for a living?

Write a sentence or so about how you feel about each of these statements and keep them somewhere safe. Re-read them after reading the rest of the book and see if your perspective has changed.

Trading is often quoted as the hardest way to make an easy living, but as we saw earlier, that may or may not be true.

We may often picture an ideal scenario that we think would be how a professional trader spends their life. Perhaps we would like to experience it.

That might involve lying around all day in your pjs, turning on the PC and the sports channels just before the racing starts, placing a few trades, banking the profits and then getting on doing something that you really enjoy.

Unfortunately, like lots of things that look desirable to us, what we imagine, often doesn't match the reality.

It again comes back to how we think.

Getting Rich Quick

If you discovered trading after being a gambler you will have a major obstacle to overcome, well more of an experience really, which someone who is completely new to it all won't have, and that is the thrill of a big win

You need to get over that one immediately, as it will hold you back. Not necessarily in the way you expect. If you have spent any length of time gambling, you will probably be used to feeling elated after a good win and deflated after a severe loss. You might think that is natural. But in reality, it is only natural if you have programmed yourself to react that way.

In trading, there is definitely room for big wins, but long-term profitability comes from regular small wins and even smaller losses. This was an area where I struggled the most. Being so used to the trials of gambling regularly, I found it difficult to accept that small profits and even scratch trades were perfectly acceptable and quite often the quickest way to success. I would usually look for a way to make more green instead of being happy with what I had already achieved.

Thinking that there is some kind of holy grail of trading out there to discover and be changed for the better by, is just a fantasy. We are all so much more capable than that.

Another of those trading paradoxes. We are drawn to trading for the money, but then we place too much emphasis on it, and it hinders us. The way out of this loop is seeing how we create our own reality.

Big changes in your whole trading life can happen in an instant. All it takes is one new thought. This doesn't mean you can sit back with your feet up and wait for it to appear though.

One of the main reasons we can find trading so difficult is because of all the apparent contradictions we encounter as we learn. Things get easier when we see that we are the creators of them.

If you can catch yourself as you are about to react to what you perceive as a bad trading position, allow yourself some time to evaluate and then respond.

Winning money doesn't create long-term well being. It seems like it can make us feel good, or make us feel bad. It does neither.

Don't try to build a framework of certainty around uncertain events. That just leads to frustration. Adaptability is essential to successful trading.

Change things up a bit. When you think you have found the perfect trading angle, remember that you haven't. Try executing it in the opposite way and see what happens. Keep things interesting.

Interests and pastimes that don't involve betting markets, daily enjoyable exercise, a healthy diet, deliberate relaxation and enough sleep, will all help improve your trading.

Understanding that we can't always win is one key to trading successfully. No one knows for sure when the losses will occur, so accepting that totally will reduce the need to win mentality.

How you feel after a trading session is a much more reliable indicator of whether it is worth your time than the profit or loss.

There are many ways to view a market. Choose one that makes you feel good.

The odds on a screen are neutral.

Trading without emotion is impossible unless you are a robot. Seeing that feelings are a response to thoughts means we have a choice about which ones we focus on. That allows you to be less of an automaton.

Minds don't have states. We can only ever feel our thinking in a moment. So the right state of mind for trading is always present. Thoughts just hide it from us.

Now isn't a fixed position in a constant stream of time that we call the present. Holding on to every now isn't the goal.

Accept that we only ever perceive, in relation to what we already know, and let the now reveal itself.

We perceive in relation to what we have already learned. It's not something we need to stop before we can become enlightened.

Once we see we are creating our own perception, our perception changes. Not for the better or worse, that itself is a perception.

We don't become awareness when we reach a certain point with our thinking. Awareness is that which is aware of everything, including what we think.

Don't think about your thinking, just observe it like you would look at someone else.

We don't need motivation or self discipline to make us do something we love to do. Open yourself up to the possibility that what you think might not be true.

Disappointment is a feeling that results from thinking that a set of circumstances that you imagined would have enhanced your life don't

Fulfillment results from a particular set of circumstances aligning with your imagined ideal scenario.

A set of circumstances, be they judged as good or bad, can only affect our lives in alignment with how much importance we place on those circumstances and how much difference we assume they will make to our lives. That we have constantly striven to find those circumstances for much of our lives often goes unnoticed. Addictions are a compulsive way of trying to change our inner life by manipulating something outside ourselves.

Don't act out of habit, act with intent.

The secret is there is no secret, so you can safely stop searching for one. That one realisation alone will save you loads of time.

There's no magic formula that you need to be successful. No one can tell you what you need to do and how to do it. Look at all courses and programmes that the adverts tell you must follow to be a success. Use these as guidance only. You can never follow the exact steps that another person took and be as successful as they are. Those steps worked for the teacher at a particular time and a particular place. Success is not a destination, it's a moving target, and a depends on our state of mind at a certain moment.

Success depends on the criteria that you measure it by. Why else do millionaires kill themselves and poor people live happily?

Our physical bodies operate within certain boundaries. There are no limits to mind and what is achievable.

We all fluctuate between happiness and sadness throughout our whole lives. We make what are sometimes earth shattering decisions, based on the flimsy evidence of a moment.

Don't pick sides. We are all drawn towards things we agree with and away from those we don't. If we spend our life doing that, we will not progress. Learn without paying attention to and comparing the new information with what you already know. This will probably seem difficult, but like anything, once you have an insight into the truth of the statement, you can't be fooled by your prejudices again. Real growth is easier then.

Meditation doesn't need to have a point to it. Just do it.

We don't have to force things to happen. Trying to manipulate circumstances to fit in with what we think will be best for us just won't work. Getting out of our own way and relaxing into the flow will yield much better results with less effort.

How we feel never depends on any one thing.

We must take total responsibility for everything that happens to us.

A truth is a truth. What we think about it is irrelevant.

Choose carefully which thoughts you believe. None are yours until you decide to own them.

Relax, imagine, and believe.

How we react to thought is the difference between us.

Identifying with limits that we have learned to accept as truth is like living in a prison with invisible locks and bars.

Whatever we think doesn't need to be adapted to fit in with what we believe to be true. Ignore thoughts, as they have no bearing on what is actually the truth.

Trying to figure things out has become so natural to us we believe it's the only way to react to what we think. Try being open to the fact that we may be wrong.

What if happiness doesn't need to be searched for? What if it hides in plain sight?

Thinking about what we are thinking inhibits the natural flow of life.

Focusing on an outcome that we have assumed to be favourable for us will only mean that we are less likely to enjoy the journey of trying to make it happen. How do we know we are correct about the outcome being favourable? Maybe it would be better to forget about the end point and concentrate on all the points along the way.

How we respond to any set of circumstances completely depends on the exact thought we have about those circumstances.

Our emotions have nothing to do with reality. They are our opinion of the significance of a thought that we had about how we should feel, based on an imaginary scale of good to bad or happy and sad. Whatever we feel has nothing to do with the thought. It's purely our learned reaction to it.

We are all constantly feeling our thinking. Problems arise when we believe our feelings cause our thinking.

Slow progress is better than no progress.

Impatience is a profit killer.

Think what you like, but only believe the thoughts that feel right.

Don't ignore your health in the pursuit of green figures on the screen.

Give your muse a nudge and yell, "it's time to create."

Money can't buy me love, or happiness.

What if everything you know about how the world works isn't true? Wouldn't that be funny?

Change for the better, or worse, can happen in an instant. Choose what you believe based on the feeling it gives you.

Constant practice will make you more proficient. Whether that will improve your life or make it harder is up to you.

Doing things compulsively won't result in feeling good in the long run.

What if our natural state is peace and happiness?

Struggling to reach a point where you think your life will be perfect is exhausting. Stop doing it, there's no such place.

Monetary goals aren't all they are cracked up to be.

Set goals by all means, but don't make your happiness dependent on them and remember that they have no power over you. You have the power, as you can change them.

I have made peace of mind my number one goal in everything I do. It hasn't half made life easier.

Keep your goal in mind, but not so much that your happiness is reliant on it.

Make goals, work towards them, but make sure you enjoy the journey.

Make goals that you will enjoy working towards, not just because you have been told it's what you should do.

Goals are a moving target. Have fun stalking them.

Just because you have set a goal, doesn't mean you can't change it if it looks like it needs to be changed.

Changing how you think about what you think isn't difficult when you can see how it really works.

It ain't what we think, it's the fact that we think it.

We don't need to figure everything out before we move. We can enjoy learning on the job

Overthinking isn't a thing. We can only ever think one thought at a time. That thoughts change faster than the speed of light makes it seem like we are overdoing it.

Slow down. We aren't in a race.

Always remember that no matter what you think about yourself at any moment in time, be it good or bad, isn't true.

Look after yourself. Eat well, move a lot, breathe deeply, help others, pick your battles carefully. And, LOOK AFTER YOURSELF.

Meditation, mindfulness, breathing, conscious calming all have their benefits, unless you focus on those benefits. Then they can become a chore.

Don't strive. Be.

Everything we ever feel is our responsibility. We carry the can, whether it's full of gold or full of horse shit.

Visualisation is simply the process of seeing what isn't there.

Find a strategy that you are happy with, stick to the rules and enjoy working with it. It has to be fun or why bother?

Self improvement is a misnomer, attitude improvement though...

Be patient in the markets and enjoy yourself.

We'll all be dead soon, so living like we are dying makes perfect sense.

Plan for the future if you must, but don't forget to enjoy now. There are no pockets in shrouds.

We aren't living in the world, we're living in a world.

No two people see the markets in the same way. Interpretation creates their appearance for you.

Blind faith isn't very logical.

Responses are individually unique. Get used to it.

Realisation of how reality is created makes life a lot easier.

Let's not get too bogged down in the theory of living. Just live.

If you aren't having fun doing what you are doing, stop doing it.

Doing stuff because you think you should will be more of a struggle than doing it for the fun of it.

Meditation is not something we have to 'do', it's a natural state that we enter and exit throughout our lives. Just like sleep, trying to force it to happen usually makes it more difficult to achieve.

Most self-help books have strategies, techniques, exercises etc to help you change your life, attitude, behaviour etc. All can be useful in the short term. Long-term change doesn't rely on such routines, it's much, much easier than that.

Self belief doesn't need to be a struggle to achieve. We are all born with it and never lose it. It's just hidden. Rediscovering it is simply a case of getting out of our own way.

Motivation doesn't need to be cultivated. Make the journey to whatever you are doing fun and you'll never struggle with procrastination again.

Starting your day with a gratitude attitude is a cliche for a reason. Don't dismiss it because it's familiar. Just do it.

No matter what it is, you won't struggle if you enjoy it.

One person's success is anothers failure.

Thinking that we can control our thinking sure can cause us a lot of distress. Really seeing that it is impossible frees us.

The sooner we stop trying to make the world fit into our recipe for success, the more successful we become.

The now is indescribable with words as it's gone before we even think about what to say.

We are told that we have a conscious and a subconscious mind, but where is the we that has them?

Nothing will change unless you change it. Do not sit down and feel sorry for yourself, no matter how hard things get. Look at the positive, move forward and put the effort in. Good things happen when you act with faith.

There is truth and there's opinion. There's an opinion about a truth and there's truth about an opinion.

You weren't born unlucky. No one is any more lucky than anyone else. Like a lot of things that we believe, it may seem so, but it is purely perception based on our experiences of life so far.

Nothing outside of us has any power to make us feel a certain way.

Keep your thinking fun.

Profit and loss have no power. All the power is with us. We are so much more powerful than we give ourselves credit for. The cases of massive change that we see are proof that how we are at any moment isn't permanent.

You'll know when you have found the hardest part of a task. It's when you are telling yourself it's time to pack it all in. Use it as a starting gun.

There isn't any pressure on us to be successful except for that which we have created ourselves. Now that is a relief.

Success isn't anywhere out there. It's a feeling and knowing that makes our experience of life so much sweeter.

Thoughts aren't right, wrong, good, bad or indifferent. The only solidity they have is that which we give them, by judging them on a scale that we created.

None of us are powerless. We have all the power that we can ever need. Any barrier to accessing that universal well of limitless opportunity is entirely fictional. It's a personal creation built on the limited information that was available to us before we realised that there are no limits.

Try just doing and don't analyse your feelings. They'll soon change anyway.

Don't try to change people's minds, to get them to think the way you do, because your way of thinking is the best. We are all on different rungs of the ladder of perception. No rung is better than any other, they are just different heights.

It might also pay to remember that our own human weaknesses are only a perception, we have no limits. And the market is simply information.

Changing our thinking isn't necessary. Notice it and watch it change all by itself. Have fun.

We can't think two thoughts simultaneously, so when we focus on one, what has happened to the one we were previously aware of?

An emotion can't exist without thought. Realising this allows us to see that we don't need to push through, or struggle to deal with emotions. If we wait, we'll soon feel differently as we respond to a different thought.

The way we see the world isn't how it is, it is how we think it is. Therefore, we only have to think differently about thought, to change it. Happy days.

Knowing how your reality is formed doesn't mean you become immune to life's challenges.

Anything we believe that's based on what we think is inherently flawed.

Trying to make ourselves feel better is totally unnecessary when we realise how feelings come about. We are all mentally perfect, despite what we think.

Imagining yourself lying on a mortuary slab will probably evoke stronger feelings than lying on a beach. Ask yourself why that is when neither is actually happening.

Life only works one way, from the inside out. Save yourself some energy by not trying to shoehorn life into compartments that your temporary thinking created. The categories that we make aren't solid.

Feelings don't need to be fixed, they change all by themselves. Addiction and damaging behaviour can result when they change at the same time as we are doing something. It is so easy to connect the two and think the action caused the feeling. It doesn't.

We judge our thoughts based on our beliefs, most of which we have inherited.

Our experience totally depends on how we judge our thoughts. A whole new experience is only ever one thought away.

Don't analyse your experience. It can't be done in any useful way, as what we deem as useful changes by the nanosecond.

Does matter matter?

Where are our memories stored?

Each of us is living in a world of our own creation.

None of us need fixing. We all have our own truth. Trying to manipulate the world to conform to a framework that we ourselves have created is both exhausting and futile.

When do lines on a page become a drawing? Art?

When do parts of a body become a person?

Realise that each of us is pure consciousness and nothing more and nothing less. We do not need to strive to improve anything about ourselves. We are pure. Looking after our body and staying active can make it easier to experience a feeling of well-being, but again, if we place too much emphasis on the self-improvement part, then the activity becomes just another something to hang our happiness on.

When we realise, we are not simply a body that lives a life for so long and then dies and disappears, our experience of life changes. We are consciousness and no amount of manipulation of outside circumstances can improve on it.

Trying to figure out what consciousness is tiring and pointless, so don't bother.

We are simply consciousness. We have identified with a body, that which we call me, since birth and been taught to believe that is who we are. It isn't.

Consciousness is all that we are. Nothing else matters, our body is temporary, consciousness is infinite.

Consciousness has no limits, any description we can give it, is governed by the language we have developed over the ages of living without the realisation of it and our actual vastness.

The human body which we identify so readily with is a creation that allows us the chance to experience consciousness, as soon as we realise that personal, physical limitations and impairments are irrelevant.

We live in a self-created world and there's not a better one just out of our reach and all we need to do is find the door to it. Consciousness is infinite and contains everything, including our view of our reality.

Mind, consciousness and thought. All three must be present for a human experience.

The consciousness we were born into is exactly the same now as then. The only thing that is different is how we have learned to interact with it.

Success is an inside job.

Comparing ourselves to others is worthless. No one's reality is superior or inferior to anybody elses. Differences are part of the design.

Thought isn't a thing that we can be measure against a benchmark of normality. Each thought is alive for fractions of a second and then replaced with another. Choosing certain ones, from the thousands that we have every day to hold on to, is a judgement that we make based on our experience of life so far. The paradox is that the thoughts we judge are the same ones that created our experience.

There are no restrictions on what we can think. Thought is limitless. We are free to think and create whatever we like.

We can't control our thinking, only how we react to it and that is fantastic news. It frees us to choose to react in ways that create a good feeling. We are going to forget this often, of course, but it's a constant which we can always come back to.

Rather than describing what appears to our mind as thinking, we can look at it as becoming aware of a thought. There is no effort involved. It's not a struggle to change thoughts. They change, whether we want them to or not.

How people think about you has nothing to do with you.

Thinking is effortless. We are conscious and so we think. It sometimes feels like a struggle as we try to hold on to the thoughts that we judge to be the best one's. Regardless of how we rate them, thoughts are neutral.

How we feel depends entirely on our response to whatever thought is in our head at that given moment.

Memories are thoughts that only spring into our present reality if we focus our attention on them.

We don't have to act on any thought we have. Get used to pausing before acting, to give yourself time to remember that.

Your thoughts arise independently of you. You are the observer. You have a choice, not about what you think, but about whether you act on those thoughts.

Never forget you are in control of how you respond to a thought. Life is easier then.

Confirmation that we have made the right decision is always easier to find than reasons we could actually be wrong.

Just because we have thought a certain way for a long time, doesn't mean that we can't change, and think the exact opposite at any moment. Thoughts aren't permanent.

Missed penalties, dodgy VAR verdicts, bad rides and missed opportunities can't make you feel bad. Your thinking is totally responsible for how you feel.

Everything we experience is because of our response to a thought, no exceptions.

There's a power behind the brain.

We humans are all in the same boat, all of us trying to steer a course to peace using whatever external help we can. The problem is often, the things we think are helping are hindrances in disguise.

We are all experts in the flaws of other people, but have difficulty seeing our own.

One correct thought can change the world faster than anything. You'll know its correct if the feeling it creates is nice.

We can't help others without first realising that none of us have all the answers.

Pointing people towards the truth is far more effective than trying to force them to match a criterion that is created by anothers thought.

Feeling compassion doesn't mean we have to allow people to do as they please if it's hurting others.

Total change can happen in an instant.

Compassion can be mistaken for weakness by people whose reality is reactive.

Give up thinking about getting rich quick. The thoughts of how much better your life will be if you get money quickly are where the problems lie. Life is how you think it is, always.

We are told change is difficult; it isn't. We are told harmful habits are hard to break; they aren't. One thought is all it takes, then life can totally transform.

ONE THOUGHT IS ALL IT TAKES.

The reliance on seeing an immediate return on what we see as a large investment, be it time, money or anything else, is just one way our thinking holds us back.

The secret to happiness is that there is no secret. A perfectly calm, serene, and happy life is always available. Sometimes we realise this, but most of the time we don't.

The search for fulfillment, whatever that is to you personally, ends with the realisation that it isn't hidden from you at all. It's with you all the time. You just didn't see it. So relax and stop struggling.

The easier life that we all are looking for isn't found by searching for it. It appears when we stop looking.

We can only find success in any field when we don't strive, strain and struggle to grab it. It's there, waiting patiently to be uncovered.

Success isn't a destination. It's all around you and always there. Enjoy what you discover on the way to finding it. We may struggle because it seems like that's the only path to success. We will think that way if that is what we have heard since birth. The most successful have learned that it is a total fabrication.

When we identify with a label, we are prone to division.

On your daily to do list, be sure to write EXERCISE in capital letters.

Always remember that you make up your view of yourself, and so does everybody else.

Everyone's definition of success is different, but they all have one thing in common. They are self created.

There's only now, so don't forget to stop striving for a while and appreciate it.

Don't waste anymore of your precious time on trying to change the way you think. It's impossible to figure out which way is best.

Everything we do, we do in an attempt to make ourselves feel better.

Our feelings are our own infallible barometer of how we are thinking from moment to moment.

You could die today, so make sure you enjoy every second of life.

Don't make the simple complex.

We create our world with our thinking. More thinking won't change it.

Happiness is simply the absence of negative thought.

Start every day by making the decision that it's going to be a good one. We all have that ability, despite what we think.

You'll know if your habits are good for you by the way they make you feel. If you feel bad after them, stop.

Trust your feelings, they are the barometer of your thinking.

Even if you are sceptical about thought creating your reality, there's no reason to behave in a way that makes you feel bad.

Searching for shortcuts often takes a long time.

Physical addictions have their roots in habitual thought, that's all.

The only reason we repeat behaviour that causes us mental pain is in the mistaken belief that it will make us feel better at some point. Never forget that beliefs can change. They are never permanent.

When we have an urge to indulge in something that usually causes us unease, try to see it as an early warning that we are out of balance and our thinking is trying to steer us back. Do nothing until you feel better.

It's ok, you don't have to figure out what's causing you to feel bad. It's what you're thinking and it will change if you wait a while.

It's not compulsory to feel unhappy with our present circumstances to be motivated to change them. Unhappiness can often mean our motivation to do anything suffers.

Feeling unhappy, results from thinking unhappy, not vice versa.

A daily dose of gratitude is a good pick me up.

Stressful thinking, which creates the feeling of stress, is more likely to appear when we understand something intellectually, without also realising it insightfully at a deeper level.

Losses litter the path to success.

Habitual thinking is the foundation of every unwanted behaviour.

Losses aren't a failure on our part. Any edge has a pattern of wins and losses that we are unaware of. Accept that as a certainty and follow your plan, regardless of where you are in that unknown pattern.

There's a vast difference between knowing something intellectually and insightfully knowing it as a certainty. Realising that difference creates our ah! ah! moments.

Don't waste anymore time trying to make your thinking better. It's exhausting. We can't control what we think, only how we respond to it.

The advice to work on your mindset is well intentioned, but unnecessary. Just be aware that we have a choice on which thoughts we give significance to.

Trying to change the way we think is exhausting and pointless. Our response to what thoughts appear is the part we have control over and as we change our response to them, the thoughts will change without all the effort.

Don't try to figure out which way the market is going to go. It's unnecessary. Respond to the figures in front of you and with experience you'll get better at predicting movements correctly.

Don't waste any time on what might have been. Concentrate on now.

Please yourself first. You'll please others as a consequence.

Thinking is compulsory, acting on the thoughts is optional.

Life can change in an instant. Not realising or remembering it causes the difficulty

Trust how your thinking makes you feel. It's much more reliable than the content of your thoughts.

What you think, is much less important than how what you think makes you feel.

Whether you think you're right, or you think you're wrong, you're right.

How about persistent, perfect practice with nothing at stake?

Losing our mental equilibrium is never a result of any outside circumstance. It's always an inside job.

We all think differently, so we all experience a distinct reality. That only becomes a problem when we think ours is the correct one and try to make others think the same.

Thought creates our reality, then denies it.

Get used to questioning your thinking. We find it easy to do with other peoples, but not our own.

Time spent looking at markets without a financial involvement is always worthwhile.

None of us can see into the future yet, even though our thinking constantly tells us we can.

Perceive it and then achieve it.

Every person on the planet is doing the best they can, given the understanding they have.

Needing to be right all the time will lead to mental discomfort.

The law of attraction is misunderstood. Wishing and hoping for something really, really hard, isn't enough. Rename it the law of action and start from that premise.

You can't fool your thinking.

Doing what you have always done and getting what you've always got is fine, if you enjoy both.

If you think you can, or think you can't, you're thinking too much. In fact, we pretty much always think too much.

It's not what we think that causes us problems, it's that we think.

Stuffed olives, to me, taste horrendous. To my wife, they are manna from heaven. To our dog, they are just something to swallow. Whose opinion is right?

Doing things because we want to always feels better than doing them because we have to, even if the outcome is the same.

Seeing that my thinking about a situation and not the situation itself was causing my mental pain was a breakthrough for me.

At the start of every day, remind yourself that today is a great day to be alive. Of course you knew that already, but remind yourself anyway.

Be very wary of any promise of free money. Most people think that happiness depends on having lots of it, so the unscrupulous always use it as a weapon.

There isn't a get rich quick scheme hidden in the exchange markets. Don't waste anytime looking for one.

We don't have to search for peace of mind outside ourselves. We only need to rediscover it. It has gone nowhere. We just cover it up with layers of thinking.

There are no good or bad thoughts. There are thoughts and there's thinking.

There isn't one world out there that we each react differently to. There's a world that we create, that we react to as though it's out there.

What accounts for the seemingly miraculous changes in people's lives?
Losing huge amounts of weight, stopping smoking after years of trying, finding God and turning a life around. All can seem to be magical. It's a new insight that triggers them. Everyone is capable of such changes. One thought is all it takes.

When we truly see that our feelings result from our thinking, we are free to enjoy all experiences without the need to rely on them for happiness.

We can kiss goodbye to any unhelpful behavior with the realisation of how we create our own reality.

Meditation can be helpful to calm us down, but we don't have to rely on it for our well being. We are always well, only our thinking tells us otherwise.

We are a clear blue sky, our thoughts are the weather. We don't have to change anything. It is always changing. That's just what happens.

Meditation is the act of trying to ignore our thinking so we can feel peaceful again. If this seems difficult, just wait. The trying is causing the problem.

Telling yourself that you can't do something isn't a fact. The fact is, you just haven't learned how to do it yet.

There are no limits to what we can achieve. Thoughts and beliefs are all that make it seem that way.

Wanting to improve in anything we do is a noble pursuit, but we don't need to struggle. Change doesn't need to be about improving ourselves when we realise we are fine no matter what.

Practice doesn't make perfect if we practice the wrong things.

Lots of us are told from our early days that life is a struggle and we must constantly strive to get better at whatever we do to be successful. The only reason we were told this is because that is how it looked to our teachers at the time and they were trying to help us. What if there is another way? One that doesn't involve a constant battle with yourself about what is the fastest way to get good? What if you could change your life without struggle, effort, or heartache? You can.

Our thinking is often habitual.

Everyone is doing the best that they can at every moment.

What happens as you are waking up from sleeping? You slowly become aware of the outside world. What allows you to experience this? Your thinking.

We are only ever one new thought from experiencing the world completely differently.

Life doesn't just happen, and we observe it. Thoughts create our world and then say it wasn't me.

We are all completely whole. Only thinking tells us we aren't.

Once we really see where our experience is coming from, life gets easier.

What if being in the zone was your natural state, and it was your thinking that hid this from you? Just a thought.

You don't have to sit on a cushion and have perfect quiet to reach a meditative state. Repeat this often. "I don't have to create anything using thought. I know that whatever I want to create doesn't involve all the effort of thinking. It will come through me as soon as I get out of my own way and allow it." All the pressure then disappears.

Personal thought is limiting, universal mind has no limits. Personal thought can be painful and stressful, universal mind is neither.

Thoughts create our feelings, even though it seems like it's the other way round. This realisation alone will improve your life.

Many successful traders make a habit of recording not only their trades, but also the thought processes surrounding those trades.

Insights spark fresh insights. Keep a close watch for them. They can appear anytime so write them down immediately.

Always learn.
Be thankful.
Help others if you're able.
Don't judge.
Be easy on yourself and grow.
Above all, have fun.

On the following pages, I have included some notebook pages for you to jot down any insights and new thoughts that you have, not only while reading this book, but also when you are trading or going about your daily life.

It can be useful to make a note of these new thoughts and then read back through them after a day or two.

You'll find that doing this can allow other insights to appear.

I wish you well on your sports trading journey and hope that you discover more new ways of thinking to enhance your experience.

Printed in Great Britain
by Amazon

35784444R00056